ANIMAL
Poetry

Selected by
Robert Hull

Illustrated by
Annabel Spenceley

Thematic Poetry

Animal Poetry
Christmas Poetry
Green Poetry
Sea Poetry

Series editor: Catherine Ellis
Designer: Derek Lee

First published in 1991 by
Wayland (Publishers) Ltd
61 Western Road, Hove
East Sussex, BN3 1JD, England

© Copyright 1991 Wayland
(Publishers) Ltd

British Library Cataloguing in Publication Data

Animal poetry.
    1. Children's poetry in English.
Special subjects
Animals – Anthologies
I. Hull, Robert II. Spenceley,
Annabel III. Series
821.008036

ISBN 0-7502-0083-9

Picture Acknowledgements

The publishers would like to thank the following for allowing their illustrations to be reproduced in this book: Bruce Coleman Ltd 5, 7, 15, 19, 21, 22, 26, 29, 31, 32, 35, 37, 42; Oxford Scientific Films 10, 44; Topham 41; ZEFA *front cover, back cover,* 9, 12, 16, 38.

Acknowledgements

For permission to reprint copyright material the publishers gratefully acknowledge the following: Bodley Head and John Agard for 'Don't Call Alligator . . .' from *Say It Again, Granny*; G. P. Putnam's Sons for 'Wasps' by Dorothy Aldis from *Is Anybody Hungry?* by Dorothy Aldis, copyright © 1964 by Dorothy Aldis; Hippopotamus Press for 'The Elephant' by Debjani Chatterjee; Catherine Beston Barnes for 'Song of the Rabbits Outside the Tavern' by Elizabeth Coatsworth; 'Requiem for a Robin' from *What is a Kumquat?* by Sue Cowling, by permission of Faber & Faber Ltd; Penguin Books Ltd for 'Night Walk' by Max Fatchen, from *Songs for my Dog and Other People* by Max Fatchen (Kestrel Books, 1980) copyright © Max Fatchen, 1980; Michael Flanders for 'The Hippopotamus'; Macmillan for 'The Prayer of the Little Ducks' by Carmen Bernos de Gasztold; In the USA, 'The Prayer of the Little Ducks' from *Prayers from the Ark*, translated by Rumer Godden. Translation © 1962 Rumer Godden. Reprinted by permission of Viking Penguin, Penguin Books USA Inc; Olwyn Hughes for 'Otter' by Ted Hughes from *The Cat and the Cuckoo* (Sunstone Press) copyright © Ted Hughes; Anvil Press Poetry for 'In Midwinter a Wood Was . . .' by Peter Levi from *Collected Poems* by Peter Levi (Anvil Press Poetry, 1984); Kevin McCann for 'One Night at the Circus'; Irene Rawnsley for 'Staying On'; 'Cows on the Beach' reprinted by permission of Faber & Faber Ltd from *The Flying Spring Onion* by Matthew Sweeney; Collins Publishers for 'Our Hamster's Life' from *Rabbiting On* by Kit Wright.

While every effort has been made to secure permission, in some cases it has proved impossible to trace the copyright holders.

Typeset by Nicola Taylor, Wayland
Printed in Italy by G. Canale
& C.S.p.A., Turin
Bound in France by A.G.M.

Contents

Introduction   4

The Prayer of the Little Ducks who went into the Ark
Carmen Bernos de Gasztold   6

Otter   *Ted Hughes*   8

The Frog's Lament   *Aileen Fisher*   11

Cows on the Beach   *Matthew Sweeney*   13

Thirty Purple Birds   *Anon.*   14

Wasps   *Dorothy Aldis*   14

Pig   *Georgina Middleton*   17

Sneeze   *Yayu*   18

Splinter   *Carl Sandburg*   18

The Does   *Issa*   18

In Midwinter a Wood Was . . .   *Peter Levi*   20

Leopard   *Anon.*   23

My Tortoise   *Stevie Smith*   24

Mouse's Nest   *John Clare*   27

Our Hamster's Life   *Kit Wright*   28

Song of the Rabbits Outside the Tavern
Elizabeth Coatsworth   30

Night Walk   *Max Fatchen*   33

Don't Call Alligator Long-Mouth Till You Cross River
John Agard   34

The Hippopotamus   *Michael Flanders*   34

Buffalo   *Anon.*   36

The Elephant   *Debjani Chatterjee*   39

One Night at the Circus   *Kevin McCann*   40

Requiem for a Robin   *Sue Cowling*   43

Staying On   *Irene Rawnsley*   45

Biographies   46

Index of first lines   48

Introduction

We all seem to need animals. We need to stroke dogs, watch seals, listen to owls, draw cows, write about cats. We talk aloud to them, and in stories and poems we imagine how they would talk back to us. 'What are you doing away up there, On your great long legs in the lonely air?' the dog in one poem asks its large human-animal owner. 'I jut up my mutt,' the otter says in another, introducing himself just the way you'd expect.

Animals are close to us, but far away too, because we don't really know what elephant-thoughts are about, or what the whale's song is saying. And when we admire the leopard and the buffalo – from afar! – it's for what we don't have, a special kind of speed, power, grace. Those animals are precious because they're remote and different – and breathtaking.

But robins and ducks and mice are precious, too. Ordinary creatures, we think, not especially amazing or frightening. But they're necessary to us as well. They're neighbourly, nice to have around for a quacky chat or a polite squeak.

Reading – and writing – about animals is a way of sympathizing and going closer to them. So a book like this is a kind of small Ark, waiting to float off inside your head with animals who'll make their din and stir there.

Not every kind of creature is on board. There are no macaws or llamas, no shrews or gnus. And they're not in twos. We could have had a serious hippo to go with the funny one, but hippos take up room. But there are more than thirty birds, two cows, unlimited rabbits . . . You can go up close and have a good look and listen and sniff at them all. Then you can go outside and find some more creatures of your own, using your eyes and ears and nose . . . and then your pen.

The Prayer of the Little Ducks who went into the Ark

Dear God,
give us a flood of water.
Let it rain tomorrow and always.
Give us plenty of little slugs
and other luscious things to eat.
Protect all folk who quack
and everyone who knows how to swim.

Amen.

CARMEN BERNOS DE GASZTOLD
(Translated from the Portuguese by
Rumer Godden)

Otter

An Otter am I,
High and dry
Over the pebbles
See me hobble.
My water-bag wobbles
Until I spill
At the river sill
And flow away thin
As an empty skin
That dribbles bubbles.

Then I jut up my mutt,
All spikey with wet.
My moustaches bristle
As I mutter, or whistle:
'Now what's the matter?'

(For that is my song.
Not very long.
There might be a better
Some wetter, wittier
Otter could utter.)

TED HUGHES

The Frog's Lament

'I can't bite
like a dog,'
said the bright
green frog.

'I can't nip,
I can't squirt,
I can't grip,
I can't hurt.

'All I can do
is hop and hide
when enemies come
from far and wide.

'I can't scratch
like a cat.
I'm no match
for a rat.

'I can't stab,
I can't snare,
I can't grab
I can't scare.

'All I can do
my whole life through
is hop,' said the frog,
'and hide from view.'

And that's
what I saw him
up and do.

AILEEN FISHER

11

Cows on the Beach

Two cows,
fed-up with grass, field, farmer
barged through barbed wire
and found the beach.
Each mooed to each:
This is a better place to be,
a stretch of sand next to the sea,
this is the place for me.
And they stayed there all day,
strayed this way, that way,
over to rocks,
past discarded socks,
ignoring the few people they met
(it wasn't high season yet).
They dipped hooves in the sea,
got wet up to the knee,
they swallowed pebbles and sand,
found them a bit bland,
washed them down with sea-water,
decided they really ought to
rest for an hour.

Both were sure
they'd never leave here.
Imagine, they'd lived so near
and never knew!
With a swapped moo
they sank into sleep,
woke to the yellow jeep
of the farmer
revving there
feet from the incoming sea.
This is no place for cows to be,
he shouted, and slapped them
with seaweed, all the way home.

MATTHEW SWEENEY

13

Thirty Purple Birds

Toity poiple boids
Sitt'n on der coib
A' choipin' and a' boipin'
An' eat'n doity woims.

ANON. (New York)

Wasps

Wasps like coffee.
Syrup.
Tea.
Coca-Cola.
Butter.
Me.

DOROTHY ALDIS

Elizabeth Siemens

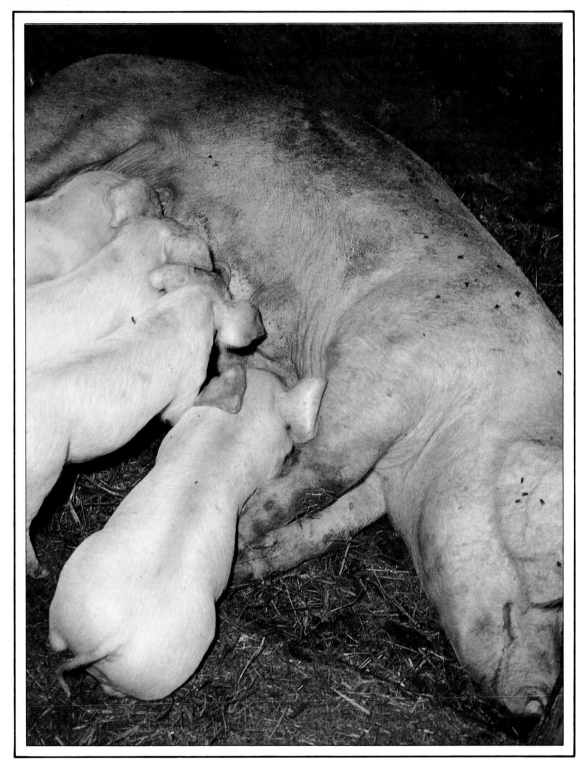

Pig

My grandad's pig, Priscilla.
Great hairy monster;
gentle, with reflections in navy-blue eyes.
Curly tail, uncurling.
Lumbering and slipping sideways in manure.
Great big matty ears flapping wildly;
pink fluffy snout,
foam of anticipation round her mouth,
snuffling and blowing meal at me,
slobbering and draining away water –
a glimpse of rows of yellow teeth.
Barging without malice
when I go to clean her out,
watching for cabbage leaves
and new clean straw.
Bristly back and flaking skin.
Neat little trotters out of proportion,
huge belly swaying,
heavy with pregnancy.
Best sow grandad's got,
very good mother,
doesn't roll on them like some.
Had fifteen last time – only lost two.

She likes to have her ears rubbed;
she almost closes her eyes
(beautiful, surprising eyes)
and grunts with pleasure,
little grunts with lots of air.
But when the food's gone
she'll start again –
indignant chilling squeals.
We go, before the volume increases.

GEORGINA MIDDLETON
(Aged 15)

17

Sneeze

Suddenly sneezing
I lost sight
of the skylark.

YAYU

Splinter

The voice of the last cricket
across the first frost
is one kind of good-bye.
It is so thin a splinter of singing.

CARL SANDBURG

The does

The does
are licking each other
this morning of frost.

ISSA

In Midwinter a Wood was . . .

In midwinter a wood was
where the sand-coloured deer ran
through quietness.
It was a marvellous thing
to see those deer running.

Softer than ashes
snow lay all winter where they ran,
and in the wood a holly tree was.
God, it was a marvellous thing
to see the deer running.

Between lime trunks grey or green
branch-headed stags went by
silently trotting.
A holly tree dark and crimson
sprouted at the wood's centre, thick and high
without a whisper, no other berry so fine.

Outside the wood was black midwinter,
over the downs that reared so solemn
wind rushed in gales, and strong here
wrapped around wood and holly fire
(where deer among the close limes ran)
with a storming circle of its thunder.
Under the trees it was a marvellous thing
to see the deer running.

PETER LEVI

20

Leopard

Gentle hunter
his tail plays on the ground
while he crushes the skull.

Beautiful death
who puts on a spotted robe
when he goes to his victim.

Playful killer
whose loving embrace
splits the antelope's heart.

ANON.
(Translated from the Yoruba by Ulli Beier)

My Tortoise

I had a sweet tortoise called Pye
Wabbit.
He ate dandelions, it was
His habbit.
Pye Wabbit, Pye Wy-et,
It was more than a habit, it was
his diet.
All the hot summer days, Pye
Wy-et, Pye Wiked-it,
Ate dandelions. I lay on the grass flat to see
How much he liked it.
In the autumn when it got cold, Pye Wiked-it, Pye
Wy-bernator,
Went to sleep till next Spring. He was
a hibernator.
First he made a secret bed for the winter,
To lie there.
We loved him far too much ever
To spy where.
Why does his second name change every time?
Why, to make the rhyme.
Pye our dear tortoise
Is dead and gone.
He lies in the tomb we built for him, called
'Pye's Home',
Pye, our dear tortoise,
We loved him so much.
Is he as dear to you now
As he was to us?

STEVIE SMITH

Mouse's Nest

I found a ball of grass among the hay
And progged it as I passed and went away;
And when I looked I fancied something stirred,
And turned agen and hoped to catch the bird –
When out an old mouse bolted in the wheats
With all her young ones hanging at her teats;
She looked so odd and so grotesque to me,
I ran and wondered what the thing could be,
And pushed the knapweed bunches where I stood;
Then the mouse hurried from the craking brood,
The young ones squeaked, and as I went away
She found her nest again among the hay.
The water o'er the pebbles scarce could run
And broad old cesspools glittered in the sun.

JOHN CLARE

Our Hamster's Life

Our hamster's life:
there's not much
to it,
not much
to it.

He presses his pink nose
to the door of the cage
and decides for the fifty-six
millionth time
that he can't get
through it.

Our hamster's life:
there's not much
to it,
not much
to it.

It's about the most boring
life in the world
if he only
knew it.
He sleeps and drinks and he eats.
He eats and he drinks and he sleeps.

He slinks and he dreeps.
He eats.

This process
he repeats.

Our hamster's life:
there's not much
to it,
not much
to it.

You'd think it would drive him bonkers,
going round and round on his wheel.
It's certainly driving me bonkers,

watching him
do it.

But he may be thinking:
'That boy's life,
there's not much
to it,
not much
to it:

watching a hamster go round on a wheel,
It's driving me bonkers if he only knew it,

watching him
watching me
do it.'

KIT WRIGHT

28

Song of the Rabbits Outside the Tavern

We who play under the pines,
We who dance in the snow
That shines blue in the light of the moon
Sometimes halt as we go,
Stand with our ears erect,
Our noses testing the air,
To gaze at the golden world
Behind the windows there.

Suns they have in a cave
And stars each on a tall white stem,
And the thought of fox or night owl
Seems never to trouble them,
They laugh and eat and are warm,
Their food seems ready at hand,
While hungry out in the cold
We little rabbits stand.

But they never dance as we dance,
They have not the speed nor the grace.
We scorn both the cat and the dog
Who lie by their fireplace.
We scorn them licking their paws,
Their eyes on an upraised spoon,
We who dance hungry and wild
Under a winter's moon.

ELIZABETH COATSWORTH

Night Walk

What are you doing away up there
On your great long legs in the lonely air?
   Come down here, where the scents are sweet,
   Swirling around your great, wide feet.

How can you know of the urgent grass
And the whiff of the wind that will whisper and pass
   Or the lure of the dark of the garden hedge
   Or the trail of a cat on the road's black edge?

What are you doing away up there
On your great long legs in the lonely air?
   You miss so much at your great, great height
   When the ground is full of the smells of night.

Hurry then, quickly, and slacken my lead
For the mysteries speak and the messages speed
   With the talking stick and the stone's slow mirth
   That four feet find on the secret earth.

MAX FATCHEN

Don't Call Alligator Long-Mouth Till You Cross River

Call alligator long-mouth
call alligator saw-mouth
call alligator pushy-mouth
call alligator scissors-mouth
call alligator raggedy-mouth
call alligator bumpy-bum
call alligator all dem rude word
but better wait
                till you cross river.

JOHN AGARD

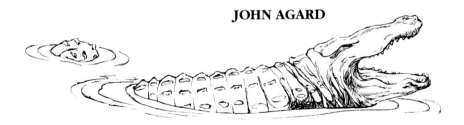

The Hippopotamus

What fun	to be
A hippo	-potamus
And weigh	a ton
From top	to bottamus

MICHAEL FLANDERS

Buffalo

The buffalo is the death
that makes a child climb a thorn tree.
When the buffalo dies in the forest
the head of the household is hiding in the roof.
When the hunter meets the buffalo
he promises never to hunt again.
He will cry out: 'I only borrowed the gun!
I only look after it for my friend!'
Little he cares about your hunting medicines:
he carries two knives on his head,
little he cares about your danegun,
he wears the thickest skin.
He is the butterfly of the savannah:
he flies along without touching the grass.
When you hear thunder without rain –
it is the buffalo approaching.

ANON.
(Translated from the Yoruba by Ulli Beier)

The Elephant

Elephants were not her cup of tea –
they were mammoth and boring,
immobile, they turned no somersaults.
Gaiety and the antics of monkeys
and insulting parakeets,
blinking and chattering,
offered her the warmth of fur and vivid feathers.
Elephants were distant, tusked and ominous.
Powerful and towering over children,
their long memories and wisdom
placed them in a different zoo for adults.

'But this is an Indian elephant,'
her father said. 'It is homesick
and will cheer up to see an Indian girl
in this wet, cold, foreign land.'
So she tore away from the noisy cages
and allowed herself to be slowly led
to greet her majestic compatriot.
She avoided those massive tree trunk legs
And looked straight up at the eyes.
A storehouse of sorrow was locked in its brain.
Tentative, she reached out a hand and patted
the incredible trunk stretched out to her.

DEBJANI CHATTERJEE

One Night at the Circus

After a plate-spinner
And before the high-wire act
While clowns throw bucketfuls
Of shredded paper
At the crowd
A cage of clanging sections
Is built inside the ring.

Silence slowly unfolds
With the net
That's tied around
Its upper rim
And through a steel-hooped tunnel
Lions enter the ring.

Quickly through another door
Comes the Tamer
Whip in hand
And CRACK
Each lion jumps upon
A starry painted box
And CRACK
Sitting up they paw the air
And CRACK
Each one upon his platform
Slowly turns around
And

In this moment's silence
A small child shouts
'Hey Mum, why don't they eat
   him up?'
And as the tamer stops
And slowly looks around
Each pair of lion's eyes
Is filled with fiery light,
Within each throat
As he cracks his whip
A rasping growl begins.

KEVIN McCANN

Requiem for a Robin

Our mother let us deal with it ourselves.
She swore she'd never have another cat.
We chose a spot beneath the apple tree
Directly underneath the branch he sat
And carolled on. We thought he would approve.
It's hard to say exactly how it felt
To take a spade and dig our friend a grave.
We smoothed his feathers down and then I knelt
To place him in the ground. He looked so small
Compared to when he overflowed with song.
I shuddered when I covered him with earth
And hoped his mate would not grieve for too long.
We sang no hymns, but knew he would be heard
Where lamb lies down with lion, cat with bird.

SUE COWLING

Staying On

Left behind by the van
which took away everything
familiar to him,

hearthrug, cushions, dish,
table scratching post, the cat
decided to stay on

but found life sharply
changed. He who had
never been much of a hunter

now flattened his belly,
crouched by holes, learned
finer skills of scent and hearing,

became animal cautious.
He could not bring himself to cringe
on strangers' doorsteps

so he came and went
through his own home cellar grating;
slept in the cold, drank

from drips and rain pools.
He took with dignity the new
harshness, lived without friends,

his only enemy the cough
which rattled his chest
and would not leave him be.

IRENE RAWNSLEY

Biographies

John Agard was born in Guyana in 1949. He became a well-known poet, and came to England in 1977, where he has worked since. His book, *Say It Again, Granny*, is full of poems made from Caribbean proverbs.

John Clare was born in 1793 in Helpston, Northamptonshire, the son of a farm labourer. He taught himself, becoming a successful writer even while working as a labourer. He had a sad life. He became ill, and spent the last twenty-three years of his life in an asylum, dying there in 1864.

Elizabeth Coatsworth was born in Buffalo, New York, in 1893. She travelled a great deal even as a child, and later wrote poems for adults and children. Her most popular children's book is *The Cat Who Went to Heaven*.

Sue Cowling was born in Merseyside but now lives in Shropshire. She started writing poems only four years ago. She has two children and numerous pets, and these supply her with lots of ideas.

Max Fatchen is an Australian, born there in 1920. He was a journalist with *The Adelaide News* and *The Advertiser*. He likes the remote parts of Australia. The outback, the rivers and the sea are the background of many of his books for children.

Aileen Fisher is best known for *In the Woods, in the Meadow, in the Sky*, a poetry collection published in 1965.

Michael Flanders was born in 1922. He went to Oxford University and was on the way to becoming an outstanding actor when he caught polio in 1943. He fought his way back to health and made a career as a famous writer of witty song lyrics. He also invented one or two ingenious gardening tools for the disabled.

Ted Hughes was born in Yorkshire. In 1984 he was made Poet Laureate. He has written many books for adults and for children. One of the best known for children (the poems started as children's poems, then 'grew up') is *Season Songs*, published by Faber.

In Japan, **Issa** (1762–1826) is the most popular of all haiku writers. He had a sad life. Stories say that he went about badly dressed, and was sometimes rude to important people.

Peter Levi was born in England in 1931. He became Professor of Poetry at Oxford. He also worked as an archaeologist in Athens, Greece.

Kevin McCann was born in Widnes but grew up in Blackpool. He has written poems for as long as he can remember and published two books for adults. He worked for twelve years as a teacher, but is now a professional writer. At present he is writing a book of poems for children.

Georgina Middleton was at school in Chichester, Sussex, and 15 years old, when the poem in this book was written.

Irene Rawnsley lives in Settle, Yorkshire. In 1988 Methuen published a collection of her poems for children called *Ask a Silly Question*, and a second book, *Dog's Dinner*, is due out in 1990.

Carl Sandburg was an American writer who lived from 1878 to 1967. He wrote many stories and poems for children. They are collected in a beautiful book called *The Sandburg Treasury*.

Stevie Smith (1902–1971) was born in Hull. She was ill as a child, and spent three years in a sanatorium recovering from tuberculosis. As an adult she was small and frail but tremendously energetic. Her poetry, written for adults, is often amusing, and was so popular that a stage play about her – *Stevie* – was produced after she died.

Matthew Sweeney was born in Donegal, Ireland, in 1952. He has studied in Germany and now lives in London. He has written several books of poems, and a book of poems for children is coming out next year.

Kit Wright was born in Kent in 1944. He went to Oxford and then became a teacher. He has made several collections of poetry for children, and written a lot for children himself; *Rabbiting On* is perhaps his best-known.

The **Yoruba** are a people of many millions who live in Western Nigeria and other parts of West Africa. They are famous for their poetry and music.

47

Index of first lines

After a plate-spinner	**40**
An Otter am I,	**8**
Call alligator long-mouth	**34**
Dear God,	**6**
Elephants were not her cup of tea –	**39**
Gentle hunter	**23**
'I can't bite	**11**
I found a ball of grass among the hay	**27**
I had a sweet tortoise called Pye	**24**
In midwinter a wood was	**20**
Left behind by the van	**45**
My grandad's pig, Priscilla.	**17**
Our hamster's life:	**28**
Our mother let us deal with it ourselves.	**43**
Suddenly sneezing	**18**
The buffalo is the death	**36**
The does	**18**
The voice of the last cricket	**18**
Toity poiple boids	**14**
Two cows,	**13**
Wasps like coffee.	**14**
We who play under the pines,	**30**
What are you doing away up there	**33**
What fun	**34**